my Dog

A SCRAPBOOK OF DRAWINGS, PHOTOS, AND FACTS

BY MARILYN BAILLIE

ILLUSTRATED BY BRENDA CLARK

LITTLE, BROWN AND COMPANY
BOSTON NEW YORK TORONTO LONDON

For Charles, Matthew, Jonathan and Alexandra — *M.B.*

For Debbie, Crystal and Rachel — *B.C.*

All about my dog

T his book is all about your dog, that extra-special furry friend. There are spaces for you to write down your dog's funny habits, and places for pictures of your dog. You'll also discover amazing dog facts and find out how to make great dog toys and treats.

So get started by drawing a picture or attaching a photo of your dog in the picture frame here. Then grab a pencil or pen and fill in the information below.

My dog

My dog's name is _____.

Nicknames I call my dog are _____ , _____ , _____.

My dog is ☐ a puppy ☐ an adult dog

My dog is ☐ male ☐ female

My dog is about _____ years, _____ months old.

My dog is as big as a _____.

The date I got my dog was _____.

The first thing my dog did when we arrived home was _____

_____.

One incredible

What color is your dog? How long is her tail? Check off the boxes here to describe what your dog looks like. There's even a place for you to draw in all her spots, stripes, and markings. What are you waiting for?

My dog's eye color is:

- [ ] blue
- [ ] brown
- [ ] other

My dog's eye shape is:

- [ ] round
- [ ] other
- [ ] oval

My dog's ears are:

- [ ] long and droopy
- [ ] short
- [ ] tall and pointed
- [ ] other

My dog's color is:

- [ ] white
- [ ] black
- [ ] reddish
- [ ] brown
- [ ] a mixture
- [ ] othe

My dog's coat is:

- [ ] long and fluffy
- [ ] wavy
- [ ] sleek and short
- [ ] other
- [ ] curly

Here is a picture of my dog showin my dog's spots and markings.

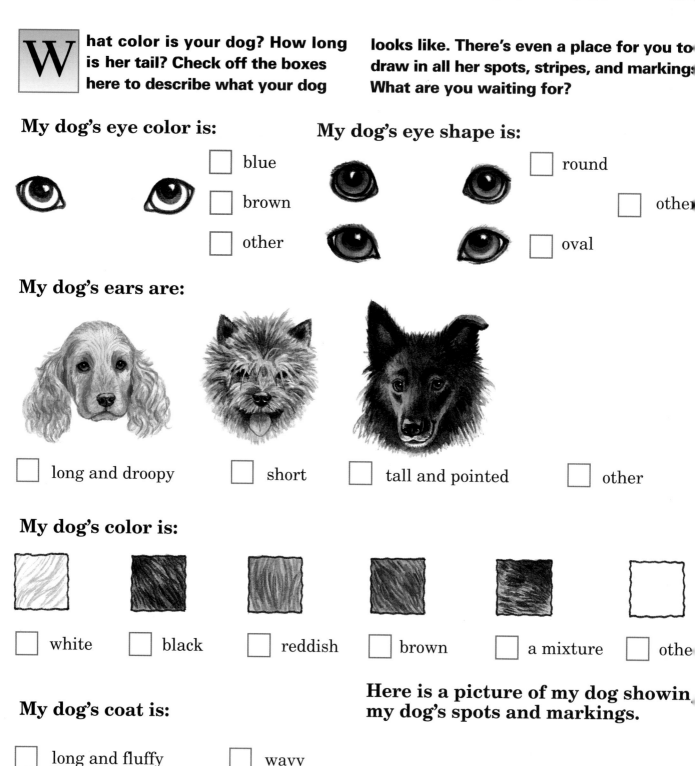

dog!

My dog's nose is:

- [ ] flat

- [ ] long and pointed

- [ ] in between

My dog's tail is:

- [ ] long and feathered

- [ ] long with short fur

- [ ] short

- [ ] other

Some of the mischief my dog gets into is
_____.

My dog loves
_____.

My dog hates
_____.

Some secrets about my dog are
_____.

My dog is so smart that my dog can
_____.

My dog's best friend is
_____.

Weigh your dog

It's weigh-in time and your dog won't stay on the scales. How can you find out how much she weighs?

If your dog is extra large, don't try to lift her. Ask your vet to weigh her on his extra-large scales.

1. Step on the scales yourself, and remember your weight.

2. Then pick up your dog and stand on the scales together.

3. Subtract your weight from the weight of the two of you. Now you know how heavy your dog is.

My dog weighs _____.

A day in the life of _____

(Fill in your dog's name here)

Dogs don't pass their time in a ho-hum way, day after day. Many things happen — but you have to watch carefully. Observe your dog for part of a day and make notes, draw pictures, or even take photos to find out just what goes on. Scientists who study animal behavior do the same things when they a[re] trying to learn how animals act.

Put a drawing or photo of your dog in each of the frames here. Then draw in the hands on the clocks to tell when he did what you've shown. Beside each picture, write about what your pet is doin[g]

Be a dog detective

Be on the lookout for each move or expression your dog makes.

If your dog is settling down for a nap, note how he curls up and where he tucks his head and tail. Does he always nap in the same spot? What happens if you give your dog a toy? Does he run away with it or stay and beg you to play? Observe your dog carefully, and have fun being a dog detective!

My dog playing

_____

_____

_____

Digging into dinner

_____

_____

_____

weet dreams

ive your dog
special security
anket for
s naps.

_____

_____

_____

Tuck into his bed an old T-shirt that you have worn but not washed. When he snuggles down to sleep, he'll smell your scent and feel cozy and content.

Fun outside

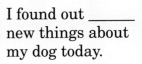

I found out _____ new things about my dog today.

I was surprised that my dog

_____

_____.

My dog

☐ wondered why

☐ didn't realize

I was watching him.

_____

_____

_____

My dog with a friend

A nest for a rest

Have you ever wondered why your dog circles around and around before he lies down to sleep? Your dog is preparing his nest, something his wild ancestors did when they found the best spot to rest. You do the same thing when you gather up your comforter and fluff up your pillow to make yourself a cozy bed nest.

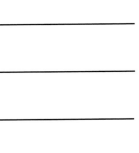

_____

_____

_____

My dog napping

Dozens of dogs

There are dozens and dozens of different kinds or breeds of dogs. Added to these are thousands of other dogs that are a mixture of breeds, called cross-bred dogs. You can see some of the many breeds of dogs on these pages and the next. Does your dog fit into any of these groups?

Sporting dogs

Some other sporting dogs:

Golden retriever
Cocker spaniel
Springer spaniel
Vizsla (smooth)

If you have a sporting dog, you can throw a stick and train her to return it to you. These dogs have been bred to help hunters retrieve their catch. **Labrador retrievers** are gentle, loving pets. Since they are easy to train, smart, and good companions, Labs are often used as guide dogs.

My dog is a

_____

and belongs in this group.

My dog might belong here because my dog looks like a

_____

Hounds

Some other hounds:

Dachshund   **Afghan hound**
Basset hound   **Greyhound**

Your dog is a hound or part hound if she has big, floppy ears, a long snout, and a large jaw. **Beagles** make great pets, but they are also raised to hunt. Long ago, they were so small that they could be popped into a pocket and carried to the hunt.

My dog is a _____
and belongs in this group.
My dog might belong
here because my
dog looks like a _____

Toy dogs

Yorkshire terrier

If you have a mini-sized dog, you know how cute and cuddly she is. But a small dog can be just as spunky as a big dog. **Cavalier King Charles spaniels** were pampered by kings and nobles, but they were useful, too. If foot warmers were needed in the chilly castles, the little spaniels were just the right size to slip cold feet under.

Some other toy dogs:

Maltese   **Pomeranian**
Toy poodle

My dog is a _____
and belongs in this group.

My dog might belong
here because my
dog looks like a _____ .

Working dogs

Working dogs help people around the world. They pull sleds, haul supplies, and search for people lost in the snow. The **Siberian husky** is strong and has a thick, warm coat for cold, northern travel. As sled dogs, huskies work well together in a team. They also make good pets.

Some other working dogs:

Schnauzer
Doberman pinscher
Alaskan malamute
St. Bernard

My dog is a

_____

and belongs in
this group.

My dog might
belong here
because my dog
looks like a

_____ .

Many more dogs

Check these other breeds of dogs to see if your dog fits into one of these groups. Even though these dozens of dogs look different from each other, they are all related. And each dog shares the wolf as its ancestor. Like a wolf, your dog is a pack animal and feels most secure in a group. A wolf pack always has a leader, and your dog also has one — you!

Terriers

Terriers, big and small, were bred to hunt. If you have a terrier, you may have noticed that your dog loves to dig. As hunters, they would chase animals to their holes and then dig in after them. **Soft-coated wheaten terriers** are popular pets now because they are bouncy and good-natured.

Some other terriers:

West Highland white terrier
Miniature schnauzer
Airedale terrier
Fox terrier

My dog is a

_____

and belongs in this group.

My dog might belong here because my dog looks like a

_____ .

Non-sporting dogs

Some other non-sporting dogs:

Shih tzu   **Lhasa apso**
Standard poodle   **Chow chow**

Non-sporting dogs vary all the way from the red Chow chow, with his blue tongue, to the white **Dalmatian**, with his black spots. Dalmatians were trained to run beside horse-drawn fire engines and help at fires. That's why Dalmatians are still called "fire-house dogs" today.

My dog is a _____
and belongs in this group.

My dog might belong here because my dog looks like a _____

Herding dogs

Herding dogs have been the shepherd's best friend for hundreds of years. As herders, these dogs are constantly on the move, protecting the flock and keeping their sheep from straying. Now **German shepherds** do more than herd sheep. They work as police dogs, guard dogs, guide dogs, and are also pets.

Some other herding dogs:

Bearded collie
Shetland sheepdog
Old English sheepdog
Collie

My dog is a _____
and belongs in this group.

My dog might belong here because my dog looks like a _____ .

Cross-bred dogs

Cross-bred dogs are a mixture of two or more breeds. If you are not sure what kind of dog you have, you may have a cross-bred. In fact, most dogs are a mixture. Cross-breds have traits from a wide variety of dogs, and some people say the result is a superior mix.

My dog belongs here. I think my dog is part

_____

and part

_____ .

I don't know my dog's group, but my dog looks like a

_____ .

Canine care and comfort

When your dog looks up at you with wide eyes that say, "I need something," she is also saying "I depend on you." Give your dog a hug and think of all the things she might want to tell you about her care and comfort.

Workout time

I love to play and exercise. Before you and I head out, I need your help. Am I wearing my collar and tags? Is your name and address on one? Do you have a plastic bag so you can "stoop and scoop" for me? Well then, hook on my leash and let's go!

Bath time

I'm probably not that happy about having a bath, but I do need one every now and again. Lather me gently with a little baby shampoo or dog shampoo. Ouch! Be careful not to get soap in my eyes. Take extra time to rinse me well because if you don't, my skin might get itchy. Towel me dry and tell me how good I am.

Tooth-care time

I crunch on dry dog food and gnaw on rawhide bones to keep my teeth and gums in shape. If you can coax me into it, you can brush my teeth. But be sure to use dog toothpaste and a soft brush. Don't use your toothpaste because I'll get sick if I swallow it.

Nail-care time

I file my nails as I walk or run on the pavement. But if my claws make a clickety-clack sound as I step on the floor, they need a quick clipping job. Ask an adult to help you, though. A slip of the clippers can really hurt me.

Grooming time

I'm proud of my coat and I like to look my best. Brush me a few times a week or more often if my fur is long. I like the hugs and the attention you give me while you stroke me.

Nap time

I like to curl up in a cozy bed that I can call my own. I need you to wash my bedding and keep it free from fleas. If you'd like to make something for me, how about preparing a one-of-a-kind dog bed?

My dog

☐ loves having her teeth brushed

☐ hates having her teeth brushed

☐ has never had her teeth brushed

My dog runs away just when I want to brush her.

☐ Yes   ☐ No

When I give my dog a bath, this is what happens:

_____

_____ .

Make a one-of-kind dog bed

You'll need:
- an old pillow case no one needs anymore
- soft, worn-out clothes or old sheets
- a needle and thread
- scissors
- a cardboard box large enough for your dog to stretch out in
- Magic Markers

1. Stuff the pillow case with the clothes or sheets.
2. Sew the open end shut.
3. Cut away most of one side of the box.
4. Decorate the box with Magic Markers.
5. Put the pillow inside and place the bed in the room that you and your family use most. (Your pet is a pack animal, so she likes to be near the rest of the group.) Show your dog her new bed, pat her, and tell her you made it just for her.

What's for dinner?

It's dinnertime and you dish out the same dog chow again. Boring, you think, but your dog might tell you differently. A regular, balanced diet keeps him active and healthy. And a steady diet of the same kind of dog food keeps him from getting stomach upsets due to diet changes. So bring on the familiar dog food! What better dinner could you serve your special friend?

What should I feed my dog?

Even vets find the many choices of dog food overwhelming. But they do suggest dry dog food over canned or moist. It's very nutritious, and crunching it keeps your dog's teeth and gums in good shape. But you can add a little canned dog food for extra flavor. Do some sleuthing and check out the dog-food labels. If you come up with a couple of choices that say they offer a complete and balanced diet, ask your vet which one is best.

What should my dog drink?

Fill your dog's bowl with fresh water every day. Always give him water with dry dog food, and be sure to make extra water available when the weather is hot.

Is there something I can feed my dog to keep his coat glossy?

A spoonful of vegetable oil or butter mixed in with your dog's food each day will make his coat shiny. If the butter or oil is too rich and upsets his stomach, cut down the amount or omit altogether.

When should I feed my dog?

Feed your dog at the same time each day, in the same place, with his own bowl. If you set a routine for your dog, he'll feel secure and know what to expect. Adult dogs need one or two meals a day. Puppies need several smaller meals, depending on their ages.

Can my dog have table scraps?

Try not to fill up your dog with too many table scraps. He needs to leave room for his healthy dog food. Don't tempt him with chocolate or sweets either, because they can make him very sick. And keep all bones out of his reach. Bones can splinter and injure your dog's body inside.

My dog gobbles down a bowl of food as big as

☐ a Ping-Pong ball

☐ a baseball

☐ a soccer ball

☐ a big beach ball

Things that my dog has eaten that were not dog food are

_____

_____ .

Dog treats

Make these delicious treats for special days. Be sure to give them out just one at a time, since new foods can upset your dog's stomach.

Be sure to ask for an adult's permission before using the oven.

You'll need:

- 2 cups (500 ml) whole-wheat flour
- 1/2 cup (125 ml) cornmeal
- 1 tablespoon (15 ml) dried basil
- 1/2 cup (125 ml) chopped parsley
- 1/3 cup (100 ml) vegetable oil
- 3/4 cup (175 ml) water
- big spoon, large bowl, flour, rolling pin, cookie cutters, cookie sheet

1. Preheat the oven to 350°F (180°C).
2. Mix the flour, cornmeal, basil, and parsley in the bowl.
3. Add the oil and water and mix well.
4. Sprinkle flour on the counter. Roll out the dough on it until the dough is about 1/4 inch (.5 cm) thick. Cut out shapes with the cookie cutters.
5. Arrange the treats on the cookie sheet.
6. Bake for about 35 minutes or until light brown.
7. Switch off the oven and leave the treats inside for a few hours to cool and become crisp. (But don't forget about them!) Save the treats in a sealed jar in the refrigerator.

Dog talk

W hen your dog nudges her nose against you or wags her tail, she doesn't need to say a word. Her whole body talks for her, especially her face, eyes, ears, and tail. Look at some of the things these dogs are saying. Then fill in the blanks and check off the boxes to describe how your dog "talks."

Top dog

Dogs don't bother with chit-chat when they meet. They get right into discovering who's boss. They often look alert, stand tall with their tails up, and try to stare each other down. They are deciding who is top dog.

When my dog meets another dog, she

_____

_____.

Once my dog got in a fight, and I had to

_____

_____.

Underdog

If your dog rolls on her back, she is giving you respect as her leader. If she rolls on her back when she is with another dog, she is saying "You are top dog and I'm the underdog."

Sometimes my dog rolls over just to have her tummy scratched.

☐ Yes   ☐ No

When my dog hangs her head and lets her tail droop between her legs, she is saying

_____.

Don't bug me!

Even some of the nicest dogs get angry. Leave your dog alone she growls or pulls back her lips to show her teeth. Dogs defend their space this way and might bite or attack.

My dog gets angry with other dogs, but not with me.
☐ Yes ☐ No

When my dog is angry, her ears point

☐ forward ☐ straight up

☐ back ☐ or _____

You're the best!

Nose nudges, touching, and close contact mean "Here I am" and "I love you." Your dog feels secure being close, sleeping next to you, or walking beside you. Next time your dog nudges you, give her a nudge back and tell her she's the best!

My dog likes to

☐ sit on my lap

☐ curl up on my feet

☐ or

_____

_____

What's up?

All senses are alert when your dog stands still listening. Her muscles tighten and her ears face forward. Her ears are receiving sounds as she is deciding what's up. Whatever it is, she's ready and set to go.

New dogs

If you find yourself alone facing a dog you don't know, stand still. Allow the dog to approach you, but don't look the dog in the eye. A dog who doesn't know you may take that as a dare. Put the back of your hand out for the dog to sniff. Then back up slowly and walk away.

My dog makes these sounds:

☐ woofs

☐ whines

☐ or _____

When my dog is listening to a sound far away, she

_____ .

My dog can do

Love comes first when you teach your dog tricks. Your pet wants to please you, so reward him with praise and hugs as he learns. If you take music lessons or play a sport, you know you have to practice a lot to improve. Your dog is like you. He needs to practice each day so he won't forget what you have taught him.

Before you start teaching your dog, put yourself in his place. As a dog, he looks up to his leader and accepts commands through eye contact. When he was a puppy, his mother looked him in the eye when she taught him. That's what he responded to. To your pet, you are the leader and the teacher. Be patient, loving, and firm, and you'll have fun learning together.

Tips to remember

- Use love and praise, not punishment.

- Start training as soon as possible.

- Be kind yet firm: you are in command.

- Use eye contact for commands.

- Repeat the same command word.

- Repeat the same hand motion.

- Say your dog's name only with the command.

- Train only for a short time.

- Practice the trick each day.

ricks!

The sitting command

ollow these steps to train your dog to sit. e sure to put a collar and leash on your og before you start teaching him anything. nd only say your dog's name when you se a command, not when you give him a colding. This way, he knows his name is eing called for something fun or nteresting, not something bad.

. **"Tags, come!"**
Attract your dog with a toy.

. **"Tags, sit!"**
Lift his chin and push down his rump so that he sits.

3. Reward your dog with a dog biscuit as soon as he sits.

4. **"No!"**
When your dog breaks the command, look him in the eye and say, "No!" Then put him back in the sitting position by repeating step two. It is important to repeat step two each time he breaks the command. He is learning what to do and what the command and hand motion mean.

5. **"Good dog!"**
Give praise and hugs for a job well done. Take time to play, and try again tomorrow.

6. As your dog learns the command, repeat these steps but leave out the food. He'll still respond to the command and hand actions.

Once your dog is familiar with this command, follow these same steps to teach him other ones. Try training your dog to sit longer. When he is sitting, say, "Tags, stay!" At the same time, raise your palm toward him and step back. Say, "Good dog!" with hugs if he stays. Repeat the hand motion and command each time he moves.

My dog doesn't like doing tricks — he likes doing other things.

☐ Yes ☐ No

Some neat tricks my dog can do are

_____

_____ .

Old habits to new

Some people say you can't teach an old dog new tricks. It's best to start at the puppy stage, but it's never too late to train an older dog.

Often bad habits come from bad training. But with love and patience you can change some of your dog's annoying habits. Then everyone will adore your dog as you do . . . and watch how happy your pet will be!

The never-come-when-you're-called problem

Often dogs don't come when called because they haven't been trained properly. And sometimes dogs don't respond because they associate "Come!" with unpleasant feelings. Have you heard people shout "Come here!" in an angry voice when a dog has been naughty? "No!" should mean "don't do it again," and "Come!" should only be used for something happy. Follow these steps and turn your pet's old habits into new ones.

1. Attach a 4- to 6-foot (1.5 to 2 m) rope to your dog's collar. Hold the rope and move away from your dog.

2. "Mich, come!"
Pull the rope a little, call your dog's name in a friendly, excited way, and give the command.

3. "No!"
If she pulls away, say, "No!" and go back to step two. Repeat until your

dog is successful. Be sure not to go o too long at one time. Dogs get tired and need a break.

4. "Good dog!"
If she comes, reward her immediatel with a biscuit, praise, and a hug.

5. As your dog learns the command, repeat everything, but without the rope and then without the food. Your dog will still respond to the command and hand actions.

The jump-up problem

Does your dog jump up on people when they come in the door? If she does, it probably happens after she's been alone and is overjoyed to see someone. Even though you know how your dog feels, most people don't appreciate the welcome. Some are even upset and afraid. Here's how to train your dog to stay down.

1. Be sure to have a biscuit in your pocket as you open the door.

2. **"Feet off!"**
   Push your dog firmly away as you say, "Feet off!"

3. **"Jessie, sit!"**
   Give her the command "Sit!" If you have not taught her to sit, show her how by holding her chin up and pushing her bottom down — see pages 18–19. As soon as she sits, reward her with the biscuit.

4. If your dog does not understand, go back out and repeat steps one to three.

5. Whenever you come in, be ready to repeat these steps. When your dog learns the routine, try the command without food. She should still respond to the words and hand actions.

Tips to remember

Use love and praise for good behavior.
Be firm but not harsh.
Never hit your dog, even if she is bad.
Say "No!" right after bad behavior.

- Use "No!" each time, not just sometimes.
- Never say your dog's name with "No!"
- Use eye contact.
- Be very patient.

Habits my dog doesn't care about changing are

_____.

When I give my dog a command, she usually

_____.

Paw prints

Does your dog tug on boots when the weather is chilly, slip on sneakers to run a race, or snuggle up at night with slippers on? No, he doesn't have to — his paws are his boots, sneakers, and slippers all in one! Trace your dog's paw in the picture frame below. Then gently examine the pads and claws on his paw and draw them in.

My dog's paw print

Boot bottoms

Most dogs have five claws on each front foot and four on each hind foot. Count the number of claws that your dog has. His claws are his handy boot treads. They grip the ground as he runs or walks. And the pads on his paws act as sneakers to cushion his feet.

Road runners

You've never seen a dog climb a tree because his claws aren't sharp enough to dig into the bark and hold him up. Your dog's claws stick out from his paws and are filed down when he walks or runs outside. Cats keep their claws sharp by pulling them back into pockets in their paws until they need them next to grip and climb.

...ocks
...nd slippers

...he tufts of fur on your dog's paws and ...etween his toes are his socks ...nd his slippers. The ...ir keeps him cozy ...nd warm. If your ...og licks his paws ...r limps, there ...ight be chunks ...f winter salt or ...mall stones ...aught in the fur ...etween his toes. ...ently feel his paw ...nd remove the ...umps and lumps.

Hot dog

Your dog's paw pads are the only place on his body where he can sweat to cool down. Sweat moistens the pads to keep them soft and free from cracks. When your dog walks along, he leaves a little sweat from his pads to say "I was here."

Make a paw print

Make a print of your dog's paw to show your friends or hang on a wall. You will need your dog's help, so be sure to find a time when he feels content and cooperative.

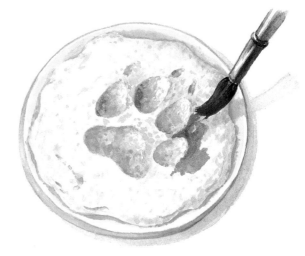

You'll need:

- 1/2 cup (125 ml) flour
  1/2 cup (125 ml) cornmeal
- 1/2 cup (125 ml) water
- large spoon, big bowl, old plastic plate that is no longer needed, water-based paints (optional), stick-on picture hanger (optional)

1. Mix the flour and cornmeal in the bowl.
2. Add the water slowly while stirring the mixture.
3. Put some of the mixture onto the plate.
4. Wet your dog's paw well and press it gently into the plate to make an imprint.
5. Let the imprint dry completely — it may take up to a week.
6. Decorate with paints, if you like.
7. If you want to hang the print on the wall, attach the picture hanger to the back of the plate.

Super senses

When you meet a new person, you use your eyes to take in information about that person. Is the person a boy or a girl, old or young, friendly or unfriendly? Your dog discovers all this news with her nose. She sniffs out the information by smelling the new dog. And by smelling other dogs' droppings or tracks, she finds out who has been by and what they were like. Your dog also depends on her hearing and sight, but she knows that her nose knows the news.

My dog's nose

Nose pad

Why is your dog's nose pad almost always so wet? It stays wet not only because she licks it but also because of moisture draining from her tear ducts. The wetness helps your dog's nose to work better. Here's how: smells drift through the air as tiny particles, and these particles stick to wet things more easily than to dry ones. A wet nose ensures that your dog gathers lots of "smell particles."

Nose print

Did you know that your dog's nose covering is different from any other dog's? Her nose print is her unique mark, just as your fingerprint is yours.

Sniffer dogs

Why do some dogs have a much better sense of smell than others? Certain dogs, are bred for their keen smelling sense. They are used for hunting, as police dogs, and to rescue people. Bloodhounds have such sensitive noses that they can follow a trail a few hours old.

ye power

ogs have better night vision than you do
nd can see even the smallest
ovement at a distance.
nd their eyes take
 a wider picture
han your eyes
o. Seeing
otion far away
nd on a wide
creen are sight
kills that are
ssential for
unting prey. Certain
ogs, such as greyhounds,
re bred for their sight and are
sed for hunting.

Let's hear it for the ears

If you see your dog prick up her ears, she
is listening to sounds, perhaps
ones you can't hear at all.
By moving her ear
position slightly,
she can hear more
clearly and tell
where the
sounds are
coming from.
Imagine if you
could hear your
friends talking from
the next street. Your dog
can! Her hearing is about four
times better than yours.

ose power

ave you ever seen a dog dig for a
easure in the ground? She's probably
nearthing a bone she buried weeks ago.
er sensitive nose locates the hidden hole
y smelling the bone under layers of soil.
Vhy does she hide bones when there is
ts to eat? Instinctively, dogs dig and hide
nings. They seem to know that hiding
od is a clever way to keep it out
f another dog's reach.

"Doggie, doggie, who's got your bone?" game

Hide a few of your dog's favorite dog
treats in a room. Be sure to conceal them
low enough for your dog to find them.
Take your dog to one of the hiding spots to
encourage her to sniff out her treasures.
Give her more hints if she needs them.
Time how long your dog takes to find
the treats.

My dog's sniffer is so good that she can
smell

_____.

My dog always hears me

☐ when I come home from school

☐ when I first get up in the morning

☐ or _____

On the move

L ook around and you'll find dogs as big as bears or tiny as rabbits. You'll find dogs that run fast and others that move at a much slower pace. But if you could peek under their skin, you'd see that all dogs share the same basic bone structure. Their bones and muscles are built for strength and motion. Look at this dog skeleton to discover which bones help a dog run.

Tail

Whether your dog's tail is long or short, it helps him balance while he is running.

Backbone

Your dog's long, strong backbone is a support for his whole body. It gives him strength and flexibility at the same time.

Hip joints

Your dog's hip joints cushion his long back legs as he runs. The large muscles that give his legs power to run are attached here.

Back leg bones

Whether your dog is big or small, his back leg bones are sturdy for running. Large leg muscles give his legs strength and power.

Knee joints

There are "shock absorbers" in your dog's knee joints that cushion the pounding his legs take when he runs. Did you know that your knees work in much the same way as your dog's?

Shoulder joints

Your dog's front legs move forward and backward as he runs or walks because of the way his leg muscles are attached to the shoulder area. Unlike a cat, your dog can't move his legs out to the side. His shoulders are shaped for forward and backward motion only.

Keep fit and keep track

Make a fitness chart for you and your dog by listing some activities you like to do together, then each day marking off the things you have done. Some might be:

- racing around the block together
- jumping over a box four times
- throwing and jumping for a ball
- running up and down the stairs

You can both keep fit and have fun!

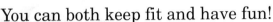

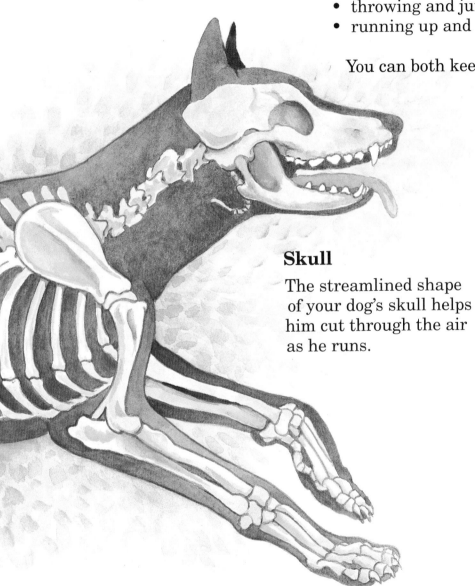

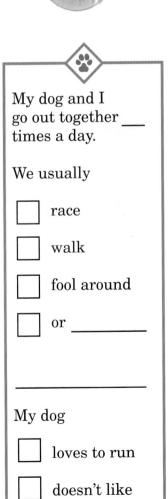

Skull

The streamlined shape of your dog's skull helps him cut through the air as he runs.

My dog and I go out together ___ times a day.

We usually

☐ race

☐ walk

☐ fool around

☐ or _____

_____

My dog

☐ loves to run

☐ doesn't like to run

Toes

Did you know that your dog walks on his toes? This gives him extra spring and speed in running. Try running on your toes. Are you any faster?

Claws

Your dog's claws come in handy when he runs. They dig in and give him a firm footing.

Vet visit

Your dog won't remind you when it's time for a visit to the veterinarian. Ask an adult to check the calendar, to telephone for an appointment, and to take you along with your dog. Save up all your questions about your dog and take them along, too. Here are some you might have wondered about.

Does a dry nose mean my dog is sick?

Yes and no! Your dog's nose stays wet with moisture from her tear ducts and from licking. When she's sick, she sleeps a lot, licks less, and has fewer tears draining down, so her nose becomes dry. But sometimes a dog's nose becomes dry and she's not sick at all.

Does my dog need to have shots?

Yes, your dog should have her shots to keep away dog diseases. Puppies need a series of shots from the time they're born to the time they're four months old. Adult dogs require shots once a year.

Will my dog have puppies?

Your dog will probably parent puppies unless you have your pet neutered. Decide with your parents if you want to look after more dogs. If your special pet is enough for you to care for, take your dog to the vet for a neutering operation. Puppies are adorable, but there are thousands born each year that are not wanted.

If my dog scratches, does she have fleas?

If fleas have set up house in your dog's furry coat, you and your dog might not even know it. Only dogs who are allergic to fleas itch and scratch. And some dogs itch because of other allergies, parasites, or dry, infected skin. Check your dog's fur often. Fleas are there if you see what look like bits of black pepper. Ask your vet what to use for the unwanted guests.

How can I tell if my dog is sick?

If you don't feel like playing or eating and are feeling tired and droopy, you know you are sick. Your dog feels the same way when she is ill. Here are some signs of sickness to watch for:

- no appetite
- listless and tired
- runny eyes
- dull coat
- diarrhea
- foaming at the mouth

If your dog shows any of these signs, have an adult call your veterinarian.

How do I know if my dog is healthy?

If your dog eats well, is active, has shiny eyes and a glossy coat, she is in the best of health. Give your dog a hug and you'll have a happy dog as well as a healthy one.

Rice is nice

Your dog may not be feeling quite right if she has had a change in her routine or has eaten things she shouldn't. Give her white rice to help soothe her upset stomach. To make rice for your pet, follow the directions on a package of instant white rice, but be sure to leave out the butter and salt. If your dog's stomach upset continues, be sure to take her to your veterinarian.

When my dog goes to new places, my dog

☐ hides under the chair I am sitting on

☐ shows off and runs around

☐ or _____

My dog

☐ has had fleas

☐ has not had fleas

When my dog gets sick, I

_____ .

Travel tips

Hooray! It's vacation time! You've been telling your dog about this special trip for weeks. As you stuff things into your backpack, you glance down to see an anxious, furry face. Pat your dog and tell him he is really coming with you. Then snuggle up with him and make a dog checklist together.

Checklist from my dog:

— Do I need any pills from the vet?

— Check that my collar is on, with my rabies tag, dog license, and ID tag.

— Bring a big bottle of fresh water.

— Carry my rabies certificate for border crossings.

— Don't feed me right before the trip. I might get sick.

— Bring a tape of my favorite music.

— I sometimes need my crate to travel in.

— Be sure to include all the things you see pictured on this page.

My dog prefers being at home.

☐ Yes   ☐ No

My dog has been on _____ trips with me.

Once he ran away and we had to

_____ .

If my dog and I could go anywhere, we would go to

_____

Pet papers

Here is a special pocket to hold some very important things for your dog.

In this pocket are:

☐ Dog papers

☐ Vet papers

☐ Vaccination records

☐ Extra photos

☐ Keepsakes

☐ Other _____

_____

Vet's phone number

_____

Dog licence or ID tag number

_____

Ask an adult to photocopy the papers you want to keep and slip your set inside here.

How to make a pocket to keep all your dog's records and treasures.

1. Fold the page along the dotted line as shown.

2. Attach this page to the back cover by taping along the top and bottom edges.

Acknowledgements

A special thank-you to Dr. Greg Usher for his expertise and generous assistance.

An appreciative thank-you to the following people: Brenda Clark for her lively illustrations; Overdrive for its creative design; my editor, Liz MacLeod, for her humor and unerring eye; and to everyone at Kids Can Press.

A warm thank-you to my friends who took the time to tell me all about their pets, and a hug for Charlie who is always there to encourage me.

Consultant: Dr. Greg Usher, Rosedale Animal Hospital, Toronto, Ontario

First U.S. Edition

Published in Canada by Kids Can Press Ltd.

ISBN 0-316-07689-9

Library of Congress Catalog Card Number 93-86660

10 9 8 7 6 5 4 3 2 1

Printed in Hong Kong